TOM DORMAN

MILITARY AIRCRAFT OF EASTERN EUROPE

(3) HELICOPTERS

Piotr Butowski

CONCORD
PUBLICATIONS COMPANY

Front Cover

With a maximum takeoff weight of 11,500kg, the Mi-24 Hind has a weapons load of 2,400kg. Its maximum speed is 335km/h; range with internal fuel and standard weapons load is 500km. The Mi-24 has a 17.15m long fuselage and a main rotor 17.3m in diameter. The photo shows an Mi-24VP. (Dmitri Grinyuk)

A normal takeoff weight for the Ka-50 Hokum is 9,800kg; the maximum is 10,800kg. It has a maximum level flight speed of 270km/h; in a shallow dive it is up to 350km/h. A normal range is 500km. The g-limit is 3.0.

Back Cover

With a maximum takeoff weight of 13,000kg, the Mi-8MT (Mi-17) has a maximum speed of 250km/h, and range with auxiliary fuel tanks of 1,065km. Its fuselage length is 18.42m. The main rotor has five blades and a diameter of 21.29m; the diameter of the three bladed tail rotor is 3.91m.

All photos by Piotr Butowski unless otherwise stated.

Editor: James R. Hill

Copyright © 1994
by CONCORD PUBLICATIONS CO.
603-609 Castle Peak Road
Kong Nam Industrial Building
10/F, B1, Tsuen Wan
New Territories, Hong Kong

We welcome authors who can help expand our range of books. If you would like to submit material, please feel free to contact us.

We are always on the look-out for new, unpublished photos for this series. If you have photos or slides or information you feel may be useful to future volumes, please send them to us for possible future publication. Full photo credits will be given upon publication.

ISBN 962-361-042-4
Printed in Hong Kong

Introduction

This is the third of a set of photo-books in which I shall present all types of military aircraft of East European countries, particularly the former Soviet aircraft.

Helicopters have been used by the East European armed forces from the early fifties, first as light liaison aircraft and a little later as assault/transport machines. Weapons began to be installed on the multi-purpose helicopters in late sixties. At those times the Soviet helicopters Mi-4 Hound and Mi-8 Hip were equipped with unguided rockets and later with anti-tank guided missiles. Czechoslovakia prepared her own armed version of medium transport Mi-4 Hound helicopter. In Poland, various types of armament were installed on the light Mi-2 Hormone helicopter.

The first true combat helicopter, the Mi-24 Hind, entered service in the Soviet Air Force at the beginning of the seventies. It has recently been replaced by Ka-50 Hokum - a new generation of combat helicopter. The helicopter combat units were re-organized in Russia beginning in 1991. Formerly, unlike the majority of other countries, Russian combat helicopter units were subordinated to the Air Force. This organization has now been changed by putting the combat helicopters under the control of the Army.

The helicopter design in Eastern Europe has been dominated by two Russian design bureaus - Mikhail Mil's and Nikolai Kamov's. Both these teams came into being in 1947. The Mil team, after the death of its initiator in 1970, was put under the direction of Marat Tishchenko. From the beginning of 1992, Mark Vineberg has been the general designer. This design bureau developed the most popular multi-purpose helicopters from the light Mi-1 in 1948, through the Mi-4, Mi-8, Mi-17, up to the present Mi-38 and Mi-54 designs.

The largest production helicopters in the world, the Mi-6 Hook and its successor Mi-26 Halo, have also been made by the Mil team. The greatest helicopter of Mi-12 Homer type ever built, which came into being in 1967, remained as two prototypes only without any serial production. Also, the first Russian specialized combat helicopter, the Mi-24 Hind, is of Mil Design Bureau origin.

Another Russian helicopter design bureau, Nikolai Kamov, has been under the direction of Sergei Mikheyev since 1974. Much smaller than Mil's team, the Kamov bureau is mainly responsible for production of helicopters which are manufactured in limited number. The longest series of Kamov helicopter was 850 agricultural Ka-26s. Ka-126s and Ka-226s are now developed as their successors.

The characteristic feature of all production helicopters of the Kamov design are the coaxial contra-rotating rotors. Despite the lack of elegance in the design, this configuration has a number of advantages over conventional helicopter design. The dimensions and silhouette are both reduced, the helicopter is easier to pilot, there is an absence of vibration in low speed flight, and the engine power output is better. These advantages are particularly relevant for shipborne helicopters.

Recently the Kamov bureau decided to break tradition and challenge the Mil team in the development of a new generation of combat helicopter. Surprisingly enough, Kamov won this competition and the Russian armed forces ordered its Ka-50 Hokum and not the Mi-28 Havoc of Mil design. Now the Kamov team produces Ka-62 transport helicopters with a single rotor, an unusual configuration for this design bureau.

The Polish helicopter industry is the strongest in Eastern Europe, besides Russia. Poles, who formerly made Mi-1s and Mi-2s from the Russian license, are now manufacturing their own original PZL W-3 Sokol (Falcon) helicopters. The specialized versions, as well as the combat ones, are now being developed from the basic utility helicopter.

Romania manufactures the Russian Kamov Ka-126 as well as the French AS-330 Puma licensed helicopters. The IAR factory in Brasov is now the sole manufacturer of Pumas. There is no progress in the manufacturing of the Ka-126 which began in 1988.

Also, the former Yugoslavia is a manufacturer of helicopters. They made French Gazelles from license and a total number of 300 helicopters have been made in several versions.

It was not my intention to present simply a set of photos. Therefore the captions can be read as a separate story containing information about the development, application, versions and characteristics of aircraft. My intention was to make this book an aid in the identification of aircraft, therefore I have presented the external differences between them. The individual types of aircraft will be presented in chronological succession.

I would like to thank all the institutions and persons who helped in providing photos or information for this book . Also, many thanks to all my friends.

Piotr Butowski

An Mi-6A Hook-A twin-turbine heavy transport helicopter displayed at ILA'92 in Berlin in June 1992. Its prototype first flew on 5 June 1957. For 11 years the Mi-6 was the world's largest helicopter, having a maximum takeoff weight of 42,500kg.

A group of Mil helicopters flying above Moscow, two Mi-6A Hooks in the foreground and an Mi-14 Haze in the background. Some 800 Mi-6As have been manufactured for military and civil use in the Rostov-on-Don factory (the first pre-series helicopters, named as Mi-6, were built by Moscow-Fili factory). The production was ended in 1981. About 500 Mi-6As were operated by the former Soviet Transport Air Forces. Some were delivered to Algeria, Egypt, Ethiopia, Iraq, Peru, Poland, Syria and Vietnam.

The Mi-6 was the first helicopter in the world to fly at a speed in excess of 300km/h. Its cruising speed is 250km/h and its normal range with 8,000kg payload is 620km. The overall length of the Mi-6A with rotors turning is 41.74m. The main rotor has five blades and a diameter of 35m. The diameter of the four-bladed tail rotors is 6.3m. It is mounted on the starboard side of a large ventral fin.

To reduce the load on the straining rotor by some 20% during cruising flight, the stub wings of 15.3m span are mounted below and behind the axis of the main rotor. The Mi-6A is powered by a two 4,101kW (5,500 shp) Solovyov/Perm D-25V (TV-2BM) turboshafts, mounted side-by-side above the cabin.

Some military Mi-6As have a machine gun mounted in the nose. It is manually aimed by the navigator.

The Polish Mi-6A demonstrates the carrying of a MiG-21M Fishbed-J fighter. Maximum internal payload is 12,000kg; the maximum weight for slung cargo is 8,000kg. The wings are usually removed when the Mi-6A is being used as a flying crane. (Zbigniew Chmurzynski)

An Mi-10 Harke-A heavy-lift flying crane helicopter in Monino museum outside Moscow. It flew for the first time in 1960. A total of about 55 have been manufactured in Rostov-on-Don factory. The Mi-10 and Mi-6 are of the same general dimensions and their power plant, transmissions and rotor systems are alike. The main differences are in the landing gear and fuselage. The fuselage depth is reduced considerably and the tailboom is deepened. The load is carried on a platform installed between the legs of tall long-stroke quadricycle undercarriage. The maximum load the platform supports is 13,600kg.

The Mi-10K (*Korotkonogiy*, short-legged) Harke-B crane helicopter is a version of Mi-10 but with short landing gear which is adequate for carrying only slung cargoes. A cockpit gondola was added under the front fuselage. The maximum sling load is 11,000kg.

An Mi-2 Hoplite twin-turbine light utility helicopter, first flown in September 1961. This helicopter can be considered as Polish product. From 1965 on it has been manufactured exclusively at the WSK Swidnik factory in Poland. Over 5,250 Mi-2s have been built for civil and military operators. More than 80% of them exported (a majority to the former Soviet Union) for liaison and training purposes.

The Mi-2URN (*Uzbrojony w Rakiety Niekierowane*, armed with unguided rockets) is a combat support version armed with two Mars-2 launchers which carry sixteen 57mm unguided rockets each at both sides of the fuselage, and a 7.62mm PK pintle mounted machine gun in rear of cabin.

An Mi-2URP (*Uzbrojony w Rakiety Przeciwpancerne*, armed with anti-tank missiles) anti-tank helicopter with four launchers of 9M14M Malyutka (AT-3 Sagger) missiles installed on the outriggers at the sides of fuselage. Note the 23mm NS-23KM cannon on the port side of fuselage. A later version of the helicopter can also carry four 9M32M Strela (AS-7 Grail) anti-aircraft missiles.

The Malyutka is a 10.9kg missile with a maximum range of 3,000m and a speed of 120m/s. The missile is wire guided by the operator in the helicopter cockpit.

An Mi-2RM (*Ratowniczy Morski*, sea rescue) of the 18th Liaison and Rescue Squadron of the Polish naval air unit. Two crewmen and a modest amount of rescue equipment takes up almost all of helicopter's carrying capacity. Only two survivors can be carried by the helicopter. A winch for the rescuer and one survivor is installed above the port side door.

A view into the cockpit of an Mi-2 Hoplite.

7

A prototype of Ka-25, or *izdieliye* (product) D, which was first flown on 26 April 1961 and first shown in public in July 1961, is seen here carrying two dummy air-to-surface missiles. It was allocated the NATO codename Harp, which was later changed to Hormone for the production versions. (Kamov design bureau)

A Ka-25B Hormone-A in the Monino museum. Production of the Ka-25 Hormone started in 1965 in Ulan-Ude factory but was later assigned to the new factory in Kumertau, Kyrgystan. About 300 Ka-25s were built, of which around 100 remain operational in CIS service. In addition, five Ka-25s equip the Indian Navy air force, nine are operated on coastal anti-submarine duties by the Syrian Air Force and others are flown by the former Yugoslavia.

Possessing maximum takeoff weight of 7,200kg, the Ka-25 has a maximum speed of 220km/h, a flight endurance of 2.5 hour and a range on standard internal fuel of 450km. The twin rotors of 15.74m diameter have three blades each. The tail unit has a central fin, a ventral fin, and two large end-plate fins and rudders which are significantly toed-in.

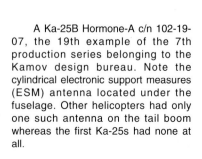

A Ka-25B Hormone-A c/n 102-19-07, the 19th example of the 7th production series belonging to the Kamov design bureau. Note the cylindrical electronic support measures (ESM) antenna located under the fuselage. Other helicopters had only one such antenna on the tail boom whereas the first Ka-25s had none at all.

A Ka-25 is powered by two 900 shp Glushenkov GTD-3F turbine engines which are mounted side-by-side above the cabin. Later versions carried the more powerful 1,000 shp GTD-3M turboshafts. The auxiliary fuel tanks are attached to the fuselage sides.

A look into the cockpit of the Ka-25B Hormone-A. Access to the cockpit of the Hormone is obtained through rearward-sliding doors, which are often left open in flight.

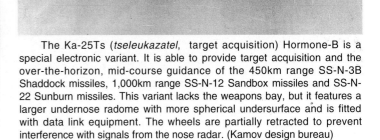

The Ka-25 is capable of alighting on water with the help of rapid-inflating flotation bags on the landing gear legs. The Hormone is not designed for everyday amphibious operations, however.

The Ka-25Ts (*tseleukazatel*, target acquisition) Hormone-B is a special electronic variant. It is able to provide target acquisition and the over-the-horizon, mid-course guidance of the 450km range SS-N-3B Shaddock missiles, 1,000km range SS-N-12 Sandbox missiles and SS-N-22 Sunburn missiles. This variant lacks the weapons bay, but it features a larger undernose radome with more spherical undersurface and is fitted with data link equipment. The wheels are partially retracted to prevent interference with signals from the nose radar. (Kamov design bureau)

All of the most interesting pictures are of the poorest quality. This photo shows the development of an attack variant of the Ka-25 Hormone with the undernose radar removed and UB-16 rocket pods suspended on the cabin sides. (Kamov design bureau)

The first flight of the Hip-A, the first prototype of the Mi-8 Hip helicopter, took place in June 1961. The photo shows the second prototype, the Hip-B which was tested in flight on 17 September, 1962. It has two new St. Petersburg/Klimov TV2-117 engines but retains the old four bladed rotor system from the Mi-4 Hound helicopter. (Boris Vdovenko)

Production of the third version, the Hip-C, was begun in 1965. The production was started at the Kazan factory followed later by the Ulan Ude works. The Mi-8T Hip-C is the standard Russian utility/assault helicopter; it is able to carry 24 equipped troops. The production of the Mi-8 and its modifications has continued up to the present. Over 10,000 have been built, including more than 2,800 exported to 55 countries. This Polish Mi-8T belongs to the Transport Helicopter Regiment in Leczyca. The helicopter has twin racks for stores on each side of the cabin, and carries a total of 128 S-5 57mm unguided rockets in four UB-16 pods.

The Mi-8's armaments load has been progressively increased and a later version, called the Mi-8TV Hip-E, has six rather than four pylons. Together these can carry up to six UB-32 rocket pods and four Falanga (Swatter) anti-tank guided missiles on rails above the racks. A single-barrelled, traversable A-12.7P (Afanasyev, 12.7 mm) machine gun is mounted in the nose. The Hip-E is one of the world's most heavily armed helicopters. (Archives)

The Mi-8TB Hip-F export counterpart of the Mi-8TV can carry six wire-guided Malyutka (Sagger) missiles rather than four Falanga (Swatter) missiles. The photo shows an East German Mi-8TB Hip-F during the Brother-in-Arms exercises in 1980. (Ireneusz Sobieszczuk)

An array of six cruciform dipole antennae is located at each side of the cabin of the Mi-8PP Hip-K communications jamming helicopter. (Wolfgang Tamme)

In the early seventies, the Klimov engine design bureau developed the new TV3-117 turboshaft engine. The engines were at first designed for priority combat helicopters Mi-14 and Mi-24. Later, they were also installed on Mi-8 transport helicopters. The Mi-8MT Hip-H came into being in 1976 as a combination of the airframe of the Mi-8 and the uprated power plant, rotor and gearbox of the Mi-14.

The Mi-8MT is exported under the name of Mi-17 as this Czechoslovakian Hip-H is designated. It is reported that the former Czechoslovakia has about fifty of these helicopters in its service.

With a maximum takeoff weight of 13,000kg, the Mi-8MT (Mi-17) has a maximum speed of 250km/h, and range with auxiliary fuel tanks of 1,065 km. Its fuselage length is 18.42m. The main rotor has five blades and a diameter of 21.29m; the diameter of the three bladed tail rotor is 3.91m.

A heavily armed Mi-8MT Hip-H. In the nose is a single-barrelled, traversable A-12.7 machine gun. On the outriggers are suspended six UB-32 57mm rocket pods. A chaff/flare dispenser is strapped below the rear end of the tailboom. Along with the infrared jammer aft of the auxiliary power unit (APU) and infrared suppressors on the engine exhausts, it provides protection against heat-seeking anti-aircraft missiles. (Archives)

This combat transport Mi-8MTV-1 helicopter has been made of an Mi-8MT equipped with TV3-117VM high-altitude engines.

An unusual outrigger with two pylons at the Mi-8MT's fuselage side instead of the typical three. The helicopter version of the B-8 rocket pod differs from the pods used in fixed wing aircraft by the elongated external tubes lined up to the front edge. In the background can be seen the flare countermeasures dispenser installed on the aircraft's fuselage.

Two prototypes of the new Mi-18 were the result of attempts to improve the Mi-17 helicopter by lengthening the fuselage. The work has not been continued however. The photo shows an Mi-18 at the Centre of Combat Fitness of Russian Army air force in Torzhok where the tests were carried out. The cockpit is partially protected by the armor plating. Infrared suppressors are installed on the engine exhausts. (Dmitri Grinyuk)

Civil versions of the military Mi-8MT have also been developed in different variants. They have been designated as the Mi-171, the Mi-172 and, as shown in the photo, the Mi-173 (Mi-17M). Note the nose-mounted weather radar.

The Mi-14 Haze shore-based amphibious helicopter flew for the first time in July 1967 and entered service with the former Soviet Navy in 1973. The photo shows the first V-14 prototype, which was powered by two TV2-117 engines. Note that the landing gear retracted into the wells and covered over with doors. In production helicopters, weight was reduced by retracting the wheels into the open niches in the fuselage. (Mil design bureau)

The Mi-14 Haze is clearly derived from the Mi-8 Hip (in the photo, an Mi-8MT Hip-H is visible in the background). New features that better suit it for its role include: a boat hull planing bottom on the fuselage, sponson flotation bags on each side at the rear, a small float under the tailboom, which provides an amphibious capability, and a large undernose radome housing a search/weather radar.

A Russian Mi-14PS Haze-C flying above Moscow. At least 230 Mi-14s were built by the Kazan plant. More than 100 are currently operated by the Commonwealth of Independent States Navy air wing. The naval forces of Bulgaria, Cuba, North Korea, the former GDR, Libya, Poland, Syria, the former Yugoslavia and Vietnam each have a dozen or so Mi-14 Haze helicopters.

The front of the Mi-14PL fuselage showing the pilot's cockpit and the underfuselage radar housing. A hoist is installed above the door. The black-winged alligator with two bombs is the emblem of the anti-submarine helicopters in the 40th ASW squadron of Polish naval aviation unit.

An APM-60 towed magnetic anomaly detection (MAD) 'bird' is stowed against the rear of the fuselage in the angle where the fuselage and boom meet. Torpedoes and depth charges are located in a bay at the bottom of the hull.

A modified anti-submarine warfare (ASW) version, the Mi-14PLM Haze-A, with the MAD 'bird' mounted in a new lower position.

The Mi-14 Haze is powered by two TV3-117M turboshaft engines which have a maximum rating of 2,225 shp. With a maximum takeoff weight of 14,000kg, the Mi-14PS Haze-C can carry 3,000kg of payload. Its maximum level speed is 230km/h. A normal range is 800km. Ferry range is 1,135km, and its maximum flight endurance is 5h56.

An Mi-14PS's nose. Two big searchlights are installed on both sides. A double-width sliding door is located at the front of the cabin on the port side.

This Polish Mi-14PS Haze-C is being used like a motor boat. Note the inflated sponson flotation bags on each side at the rear fuselage. Each of the bags has a 4 cubic meter capacity.

The late production Mi-14PS Haze-C has a characteristic fairing with searchlights in the nose. These lights can pierce the chilling darkness surrounding the survivors of a nighttime crash in the ocean.

A view into the navigator/weapon systems officer's compartment inside the cabin of the Mi-14PL Haze-A. He is seated in the armored seat in the starboard side of the cabin.

This photograph provides a view into the pilot's cockpit of the Mi-14PS Haze-C. The Mi-14 has a crew of four: pilot, co-pilot and two crewmen to perform the rescue operations.

An *izdieliye* 240, the first prototype of the Mi-24 Hind combat helicopter, flew for the first time in September 1969 piloted by Herman Alfyorov. It was powered by two TV2-117 engines and had a different wing than the later production helicopters, without deep wing-tip pylons and without anhedral. Note also the smaller cockpit windows and the lack of the anti-tank missile guidance pod. (Mil design bureau)

After manufacturing a few pre-series Mi-24 Hind-B helicopters (the first left the Arsenyev factory in November 1970), the full scale production of the Mi-24A Hind-A began. The production was later carried out also by the factory in Rostov-on-Don. The photo shows an early production Mi-24A Hind-A, re-engined with the 2,225 shp Klimov TV-3-117A engines and with the tail rotor on the starboard side of the tailfin. This Mi-24A carries four UB-32 rocket pods and four 9M17 Falanga (AT-2 Swatter) anti-tank missiles on the wing pylons. Note the SRO-2 (Odd Rods) IFF antenna on the center cockpit canopy frame. (Mil design bureau)

An Mi-24A Hind-A manufactured in the third quarter of 1972. Note that the tail rotor was transferred from the starboard to the port side of the tail fin. The IFF antenna was relocated to the oil cooler nacelle, forward of the main rotor head.

The most outstanding feature of the Mi-24A Hind-A, when compared with the later versions, is a big common cockpit for the weapons operator at the front machine gun, and a pilot behind him whose seat is shifted slightly to the port side. A third crew member, the flight engineer, is located in the passage between the pilot cockpit and cargo cabin. Note a single-barrelled, traversable A-12.7 machine gun in the nose and the bulge under the nose which houses the missile guidance pod.

Experience from flying the Mi-24A in service taught that forward visibility from the cockpit was poor when the pilot and weapon systems officer were seated on the same level. It was also decided that a chance explosion could hit and injure both of the men. In 1976, the Mi-24D (or *izdieliye* 244) entered the service with a redesigned front fuselage. The cockpit of the Mi-24D Hind-D is double-decked, with the weapon systems officer being housed in the nose. Behind and above him is the pilot. Each seat is covered by a separate bulging canopy cover.

The Mi-24A's machine gun proved to be insufficient. Therefore, the Mi-24D's armament includes a four-barrelled 12.7mm YakB-12.7 machine gun in a USPU-24 turret under the nose. In the vicinity of the machine gun is found the optical sight cupola for the anti-tank missile system on the left side, and the Raduga-F radio command guidance pod for 9M17P Falanga (AT-2 Swatter-C) missiles on the right side.

The photo illustrates the extreme position of the machine gun barrels. The YakB-12.7 machine gun has a rate of fire of 4,800 rounds per minute and a maximum effective range of 1,500m. The weapon can be trained through 60 degrees left and right, elevated by 20 degrees and depressed by 60 degrees.

A training version of the Mi-24DU (U for: *uchebnyi*, trainer). The weapons operator's post has been adopted for use by the instructor and the machine gun has been removed.

The Mi-24V Hind-E has a new armament system that includes the more modern 9M114 Shturm (AT-6 Spiral) supersonic anti-tank guided missiles. The Shturm missile rails on the wing end plate pylons and the larger missile guidance pod on the port side of the nose are the primary identification features of the Mi-24V.

Beginning with the Mi-24V, new doors were adopted for the optical sight installed in the dome under the starboard side of the front part of the fuselage. In the Mi-24D, the cover was a single-layer type. The sight was uncovered by opening the steel door. In the next version, there was an additional armored glass cover that made rough aiming possible and allowed for more accurate aiming once the door was opened. This change was made to protect the sight against impurities (dust, insects etc.).

As a result of the Afghanistan War experience, numerous airborne survival measures were introduced into the design of the Mi-24 Hind. For the first time, ASO-2V chaff/flare dispensers were strapped underneath the rear end of the tailboom. Initially, they were fastened by means of hoops. Later, factory-made attachments were used, as can be seen by this photo of an Mi-24 Hind E. The Russian inscription *OPASNO* means "danger".

The number of ASO-2V chaff/flare dispensers was later increased from four to six. They were installed in a big fairing on the side of the fuselage.

After some time, the unnecessary fairing was removed. These modifications were made on all of the helicopters fighting in Afghanistan, and the Mi-24 Hind and Mi-8 Hip as well. This photo shows the block of three ASO-2V flare dispensers at the starboard side of an Mi-8MT Hip-H helicopter.

In addition to using decoy flares and active infrared jammer, the designers have made efforts to reduce the infrared signature of their helicopters. An EVU infrared suppression cool air mixer can be fitted on the engine exhaust. The EVU system is believed to be used only in combat zones because of the engine performance degradation that it causes.

The final form of the ASO-2V dispensers, following a slight change of arrangement and after the ultimate removal of fairings, is seen on this Mi-24P Hind-F. You can also see the LIP infrared pulse jammer on the spine of helicopter immediately aft of the main rotor. Beginning in 1986, these units have been retrofitted to older Mi-24s during major overhauls.

Some of the helicopters have been equipped with the modern Bieryoza warning system, which can be externally identified by two large sensors on both sides of the nose. This Polish Mi-24V includes the many "Afghan tricks" carried by Mi-24s: LIP infrared jammer, modified exhaust stubs to accommodate the exhaust suppressor/ mixer, chaff/flare dispenser on the tailboom, and the nose sensor of the Bieryoza warning system.

A three pole SRO-2 IFF antenna is mounted on the air data boom attachment on the frame of the gunner's canopy. NATO has given the name of "Odd Rods" to these antennae.

A detail shot of the Mi-24D Hind D. The windscreen panel of the gunner's cockpit is made of a combination of layers of plastic and glass. It is designed to be bulletproof against small arms fire.

A new IFF device was fitted on the late production helicopters. When the system electronically questions the identity of a potentially hostile target and fails to secure the "friendly" electronic response, it identifies the aircraft as an enemy.

This three pole rear SRO-2 (*samolotnyi radiolokatsionnyi otvetchik*, airborne radar responder) identification friend-or-foe (IFF) antenna is mounted under the tailboom. A rear navigation light can be seen at the left.

A big fairing for the S-13 camera gun, with its round front window, is installed at the tip of the port side wing. Only the Mi-24D and the Mi-24V versions have the camera gun in this place. A Sirena-3M radar warning system sensor protrudes at the side. The port navigation light is mounted on the wing tip pylon.

A tail bumper under the rear end of tailboom. Note the strapped-on chaff/flare dispenser. The Polish inscription *NIEBEZPIECZNIE* means "danger".

An optical sight cupola for the anti-tank guided missiles system is mounted under the nose of this helicopter. The AT-6 missiles that the Hind E carries have a longer range than the TOW missiles fitted on Western helicopters. Note the armored door that is shown open.

A main instrument panel in the pilot's cockpit. At the right side there is a big screen for the cartographic display that plots the actual aircraft position for the pilot.

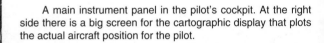

This is a study of the instrument panel in the pilot's cockpit. The pilot and the weapon systems officer each have their own different set of instruments that reflect each of their individual responsibilities.

A view of the starboard instrument panel. Note the cockpit door locking handle at the side. The pilot's canopy is fixed so he must enter the cockpit by means of steps and a door on the starboard side of the helicopter.

This photo shows a simple reflector-type PKV gunsight in front of the pilot's head. A fan is on the right side.

A close-up of the KS-53 gun sight.

An aerial view of gunner's compartment. The small control stick, enabling the emergency control of aircraft by the gunner, is seen in the lower part. The rod protruding from the starboard side is one of the pedals of the emergency rudder bar. The KS-53 gun sight occupies the central position in the compartment.

The missile control sight is mounted on the starboard side of the cockpit. A soft rubber rest for the gunner's forehead is seen on the upper part.

A view of the Hind armament. From left to right: UPK-23-250 twin-barrelled 23mm cannon pod; UB-32 57mm rocket pod; B-8V-20 80mm rocket pod and KMGU cluster bomb on the inner pylon of an Mi-24V Hind-E.

A detail view of the Mi-24V wing showing from left to right: an auxiliary fuel tank, UB-32 57mm rocket pod and a pair of 9M114 Shturm (AT-6 Spiral) missile tubes. The Shturm is a tube launched, semi-automatic radio-guided anti-tank missile. Weighting 31.8kg, the Shturm is 1,830mm long, with a calibre of 130mm. Its 6kg hollow charge warhead can penetrate 500mm of armor. Minimum range is 1,000m; maximum is 5,000m. Its flight speed is 350-400 m/s.

A close-up view of the KMGU cluster bomb on the inner pylon of an Mi-24V. Note the two racks used to carry a pair of Shturm missile tubes on each of the other pylons.

This close-up view of the Mi-24V wing shows a 9M17 Falanga anti-tank guided missile as well as a UB-32A rocket pod and a UPK-23 gun pod. (Dmitri Grinyuk)

A wing of the Mi-24P with a pair of Shturm missiles and some B-8V-20 rocket pods attached. Note the lack of a camera gun. Now the time has come to explain the meaning of helicopter serial number for the spotters. The first three figures, 353, denote the factory code. The next three, 243, are the product code. The Hind's variants have the following codes: Mi-24A is *izdieliye* 245, Mi-24D - *izdieliye* 244, Mi-24DU - *izdieliye* 249, Mi-24V - *izdieliye* 242, Mi-24P - *izdieliye* 243, Mi-24VP - *izdieliye* 258. The successive two figures mean the quarter and year of manufacturing, i.e., the second quarter of 1988 in our example. Then come the two figures of the series number (25) and the two figures of the helicopter number (84). The middle figure is without meaning.

The Mi-24P Hind-F, known since 1982, is a modified Mi-24V with the nose machine gun turret removed and a GSh-23 23mm twin-barrelled cannon pack fitted externally to the starboard side of the nose.

An unusual view of the front of an Mi-24P from below.

This Mi-24 receives a full supply of fuel prior to flight. Note the main cabin door that has one segment opening upward and one opening downward. The main cabin can accommodate eight fully-equipped troops.

About 100 of the Mi-24s are special reconnaissance helicopters, built in two principal versions: an Mi-24R Hind-G1 for nuclear/biological/chemical warfare, and an Mi-24K Hind-G2. The photos shows an Mi-24K (*korrektirovshchik*; artillery spotting) artillery spotter. Instead of an undernose optical sight and a missile guidance pod, the Mi-24K has a low-light-level TV camera pack. The four barrelled machine gun has been retained. (Wolfgang Tamme)

The latest Hind variant, the Mi-24VP, is similar to the Mi-24V Hind-E but is equipped with a twin barrelled GSh-23 23mm cannon instead of the standard YakB-12.7 machine gun.

This Mi-24 (designed for ecological research of the atmosphere) was built under the system of "*konversiya* " - the transformation of a part of Russian industry from military into civil production. (Archives)

Russian airmen use all of their ingenuity to decorate their helicopters with the national colors along with the red star, which is still the official national insignia. The Berkuty helicopter aerobatic team was established early in 1992 in Torzhok, 230km north of Moscow. Their Mi-24P and Mi-24VP helicopters have Russian tricolor stripes along the whole fuselage and colored air intake dust covers.

The first prototype of the Ka-252 (or *izdieliye* 2D) helicopter. On 8 August 1973, Yevgeniy Laryushin made the first hovering in an Ka-252, and on 24 December he made the first full circle. The fuselage of the Ka-252 is the same as that of the later production Ka-27 helicopters, but the nose with the pilot's cockpit has its origins in the older Ka-25. Also, there are no fixed slats at the leading edge of the vertical tail fins, and no ventral search radar under the nose. (Archives)

The production Ka-252 helicopters, called the Ka-27 Helix, began to replace the Ka-25 Hormone on board ships in 1981. The Ka-27 is manufactured by a factory in Kumertau, the same which formerly made Ka-25 helicopters. About 100 are currently operated by the Commonwealth of Independent States Navy air wing. Both India and the former Yugoslavia have a dozen or so of the Ka-28 export version. This Ka-27 Helix-A helicopter (shown without a fuselage number) was displayed during the air exposition in Moscow in August 1989.

The new rounded nose of the Ka-27 has extensive windscreens. Ka-27 can be operated at night or in adverse weather. Additionally, the designers were required to produce a helicopter that would fold down into much the same shipboard space as the Ka-25 Hormone. The Ka-27 is slightly larger than the Ka-25 (but its engines have twice as much power) and the takeoff weight is greater by 1.6.

The Ka-27 Helix-A is a standard ship-based anti-submarine variant, operated from carrier/cruisers, cruisers and missile frigates. The search radar is housed in the undernose radome; the dipping sonar is housed in compartment at the rear of the cabin. Weapons include either two torpedoes or eight high-explosive (HE) conventional PLAB-250-120 depth charges or a nuclear depth charge, carried inside the fuselage. The total weapons load is 2,000kg.

A Ka-27PS Helix-D. The twin rotors of 15.90m diameter have three blades each. Two 2,200 shp St. Petersburg/Klimov TV3-117VM turboshaft engines are mounted side-by-side above the cabin. The takeoff weight of the Ka-27 Helix is 12,000kg. It has a maximum speed of 270km/h, flight endurance of 4.5 hour and range of 700km. Unlike the Hormone, the Helix has no central fin but the remaining fins are still toed-in. On their leading edges they have fixed slats. Note two signal bombs carried on the rear starboard side of the fuselage.

The Ka-252TB combat transport version (*transportno-boyevoi*, combat transport or *izdieliye* D2B) was made from the Ka-27 (Ka-252). This version, after starting the production in 1984, was named Ka-29 Helix-B. More than 30 are now used by the CIS naval aviation force. The Ka-29 is designed for transport and close support of sea-borne assault troops. The ASW equipment and weapons have been removed and replaced by the weapons system taken from the Mi-24V Hind-E combat helicopter. Sixteen assault troops can occupy folding seats inside the cabin. The studies of this Ka-29 illustrate the rather strictly observed paint schemes applied on these helicopters.

Some important changes have been introduced into the construction of the front part of the Ka-29 airframe which has been made wider by about 0.5m in respect to the Ka-27. Note the three flat-plate windscreen glazing instead of the two-piece curved transparency. The flight deck and engine bay were both heavily armored.

This Ka-29, number "208", is one of the prototypes made from the ASW Ka-27 Helix-A. An oval fairing characteristic of the Ka-27 is mounted near the main landing gear. The cargo cabin doors are of the sliding type and not the upward/downward opening style as in the later production Ka-29 helicopters. (Kamov design bureau)

In 1983, a new generation of helicopter, the Mi-26 (seen in the background) began to replace the Mi-6A. As time passes and progress in design is made, all aircraft become obsolete to some degree.

The Mi-2 is an extremely versatile helicopter, able to accept a wide variety of specialist role equipment and thus undertake a comprehensive range of tasks. The photograph shows an Mi-2Ch (chemical) with contamination indicating and smoke screen laying equipment. (Waclaw Holys)

The Ka-25B (*boyevoi,* combat) Hormone-A is a standard ship-based anti-submarine version. It can be operated from carrier/cruisers, cruisers and missile frigates. The Initsiativa-2 search radar is housed in the undernose radome; dipping sonar is housed in a compartment at the rear of cabin. In a search variant, the Ka-25B is equipped additionally with towed APM-60 magnetic anomaly detection (MAD) gear and dipping sonar, as well as a cannister for 36 RGB-NM or 8 bigger RGB-N sonobuoys, which are fitted externally to the rear cabin sides. The strike variant is equipped with an underfuselage weapons bay for either a single AT-1 torpedo, four conventional PLAB-250-120 or a single nuclear depth charge. The total weapons load is 1,090kg. A major shortcoming of the Ka-25 is said to be a lack of night and all-weather sonar dipping capability.

This view of the front portion of the Ka-25B's fuselage shows the undernose-mounted Initsiativa-2 search radar antenna, the sliding door for the crew cabin and the helicopter's nosewheel. Note the Soviet Navy flag near the cabin door.

The Ka-25PS (*poiskovo-spasatelnyi*, search-and-rescue) Hormone-C is a utility and search-and-rescue (SAR) helicopter, generally similar to the Hormone-A, but with non-essential operational equipment and weapons removed. The hoist is installed at the port side; two hemispheres of unknown application are mounted under the fuselage. The Ka-25PS usually has a red and white paint scheme. (Archives)

Helicopters have assumed an increasingly important role in CIS electronic warfare (EW) operations. Two versions of the Mi-8, the Hip-D and the Hip-G, are used as airborne command posts and communications posts, as well as for communications relay. Another, the Hip-J, is a radar jammer. This photo shows an Mi-8PP Mayak Hip-K, which is a communications jamming version. Note the heat exchangers installed under the front of the fuselage. (Wolfgang Tamme)

The passenger version, the Mi-8P (*passazhirskiy*, passenger),has standard seating for twenty-eight. An executive Mi-8S (salon) version offers six to eleven seats of greater comfort. Both the versions have large rectangular cabin windows rather than circular ones like in the assault Hips. The photo shows an Mi-8S Hip-C that belongs to the Ministry of Internal Affairs of former Czechoslovakia.

An Mi-8MT Hip-H. Note the DISS Doppler navigation radar antenna below the tail boom. Above the forward end of the tailboom is installed a LIP (*lampa infrakrasnykh pomekh*, infrared jamming lamp, Hot Brick by NATO) infrared jammer. The cockpit is partially protected from ground fire by armor plating.

An Mi-14PL (*protivo-lodochnyi*, anti-submarine) Haze-A basic anti-submarine warfare (ASW) version helicopter. Its operational equipment include a large undernose radome housing an Initsiativa-2M search-weather radar, a retractable Oka-2 sonar unit housed in the starboard rear of the planing bottom and an APM-60 magnetic anomaly detector (MAD). Weapons include two AT-1 torpedoes or eight high-explosive (HE) conventional PLAB-250-120 depth charges or a nuclear depth charge, carried in an enclosed bay in the bottom of the hull.

Search and rescue Mi-14PS haze-C (*poiskovo-spasatelnyi*, search-and-rescue) helicopter has no ASW equipment or armament. It has room for ten survivors in the cabin and carries ten 20-place life rafts. The MAD 'bird' is absent and added is a small box between the Doppler radar and the rear fuselage. Note the air conditioning pod on the starboard side of the cabin.

A Polish Mi-14PS Haze-C is shown here picking up a basket of survivors from the water. All over the world, search and rescue helicopters like this one have proven their worth by performing life saving operations.

A late production Mi-24A. Hind-A entry to the cockpit is made through the hinged upward-opening cockpit side window and a rear sliding pilot's window on the port side. The crew's boarding steps are under the canopy windows. Note the gun camera carried on the upper port inboard pylon.

An Mi-24D Hind D of the former Czechoslovakia's 51st Combat Helicopter Regiment in Prostejov. Czechoslovakia was one of the first neighboring nations to import the Hind. Sources indicate that they have received about twenty-two of them.

More than 2,300 Mi-24s have been built. About 1,250 are currently operated by the Commonwealth of Independent States army air force and about 700 have been exported to more than twenty countries. This Czecho-Slovakian Mi-24D Hind-D conducts a fly-by during an air show at Prostejov airfield in 1989.

The Mi-24P Hind-F, known since 1982, is a modified Mi-24V with the nose machine gun turret removed and a GSh-23 23mm twin-barrelled cannon pack fitted externally to the starboard side of the nose.

This Mi-24 receives a full supply of fuel prior to flight. Note the main cabin door that has one segment opening upward and one opening downward. The main cabin can accommodate eight fully-equipped troops.

A Ka-27PS in stand-by mode on the Kala airfield near Baku in Azerbaijan on the coast of the Caspian Sea. The Ka-27PS (*poiskovo-spasatelnyi*, search-and-rescue) Helix-D is a utility and search-and-rescue (SAR) helicopter, generally similar to Helix-A, but with inessential operational equipment and weapons removed. The electrically-driven winch is mounted just above the port door. Emergency flotation bag housings are fitted on each side of the lower fuselage, forward of the main landing gear. Above them, auxiliary fuel tanks are attached to the fuselage sides.

The separate variant of the Ka-27 is a civilian Ka-32 Helix-C. The Ka-32S (*sudovoi*, shipborne) is the exact copy of the search-and-rescue Ka-27PS only without the special rescue equipment. The Ka-32T (*transportnyi*, transport) is a variant with much more modest navigation equipment and without the undernose radar. This photo shows the newest civil version - the flying crane Ka-32K (*kran*, crane) - which was exposed for the first time at the ILA '92 show in Berlin in June 1992.

The Ka-252TB combat transport version (*transportno-boyevoi*, combat transport or *izdieliye* D2B) was made from the Ka-27 (Ka-252). This version, after starting the production in 1984, was named Ka-29 Helix-B. More than 30 are now used by the CIS naval aviation force. The Ka-29 is designed for transport and close support of sea-borne assault troops. The ASW equipment and weapons have been removed and replaced by the weapons system taken from the Mi-24V Hind-E combat helicopter. Sixteen assault troops can occupy folding seats inside the cabin. The studies of this Ka-29 illustrate the rather strictly observed paint schemes applied on these helicopters.

An Mi-26 Halo of the Russian Transport Air Force. The prototype of the Mi-26 made its maiden flight on 14 December 1977, and production began in 1983 at the Rostov-on-Don factory. This is the largest helicopter in use in the world. More than 60 Mi-26s are operated by the CIS military transport air units. Ten machines have been sold to India.

A sea rescue version of the Sokol, the W-3RM Anaconda, in service with the 18th Liaison and Rescue Squadron of Polish naval air wing. Thanks to the inflated flotation bags the Anaconda can alight on water.

This same W-3RM Anaconda, painted in different scheme seem at Berlin's ILA'92 exposition. A retractable rescue winch is able to lift two persons in a basket on the port side of the cabin.

An assault version of W-3 Sokol, the W-3U Salamander, uses the armament system of the Mi-24V Hind-E helicopter. The outriggers on each side of the cabin carries two Polish-made Mars-8 rocket pods and two tube-launched 9M114 Shturm anti-tank missiles. A GSh-23 twin-barrelled 23mm cannon is fitted on the starboard side of the lower fuselage. (Waclaw Holys)

Polish PZL Huzar (Hussar) combat support helicopter during the tests in South Africa. It is a version of Sokol equipped with Western systems. The standard weapons include two Polish-made Mars-2 rocket packs with sixteen 57mm rockets each and two four-tube launchers of TOW anti-tank guided missiles. Huzar can alternatively carry Polish-made ZR-8 launchers with small bomb packs or other standard weapons. GA-120mm non-recoil gun is installed in rotating turret under the nose. (Archives)

A total of four flying prototypes of the Mi-28 were built (with fuselage numbers 012 through 042), and in 1993 a serial production will begin in Rostov-on-Don factory.

The Mi-28's fourth prototype, number "042", as displayed at Ramenskoye in August 1992. With a normal takeoff weight of 10,400kg, the Mi-28 Havoc has a weapons load of 2,000kg. Its maximum speed is 300km/h, and its range with internal fuel and standard weapons load is 475km.

The "012" is the third prototype of the new Kamov V-80, now ready for aerodynamic tests. It has no fire control system and lacks a cannon at the starboard side of the fuselage. The big boxes suspended under the wings contain the measuring equipment. The cameras for recording the behavior of rotors in flight are installed on the neighboring pylons.

A side-view of Ka-50 "Werewolf".

Two copies of Ka-50 are usually presented during international shows. First, side number "020" is named "Werewolf", the other one is "021", "Black Shark".

This Ka-29, number "209", shoots 80mm S-8 unguided rockets from its B-8V-20 launchers. The TV-camera for recording the test results is barely visible on the outrigger. (Kamov design bureau)

One of the Ka-29's prototypes, number "209", armed with four UB-32 57mm unguided rocket pods. Note the lack of a window for the optical sight for anti-tank missile guidance. (Kamov design bureau)

The Ka-29 has undernose-mounted optical sight window and a radio command missile guidance pod instead of the Ka-27PL's radar.

A Ka-29 Helix-B shown on the Khodynka airfield in Moscow in August 1989. In respect to the former Ka-29, this helicopter is additionally equipped with the LIP (Hot Brick) infrared jammer mounted aft of the auxiliary power unit, rearward of an electronic support measures pod.

A rear view of the Ka-29.

A view of the Ka-29's weapons pylon and the main landing gear. Note a two-part upward/downward opening cabin door instead of the Ka-27's sliding door at the rear of the cabin.

A rear part of the Ka-29's engine compartment with the auxiliary power unit (APU). A "flower pot" ESM (Electronic Support Measures) navigation light are installed on it.

A view into the cockpit of the Ka-29. An ASP-17VK gun sight is positioned above the main instrument panel. A Shturm missile control sight is visible in the background.

The Ka-29RLD (*radio-lokatsyonnovo dozora*, radar control) is an airborne early warning and control system helicopter. No stores pylons are fitted to this variant. The wheels can be partially retracted to prevent interference with signals from the lowered underfuselage radar. Note the confusing inscriptions "Aeroflot" and "Gigrometcentr" (Hydro and Meterology Center) on the fuselage. (Kamov design bureau)

The three Helix variants on board the Admiral Kuznetsov aircraft carrier: Ka-27 Helix-A (number "18"), Ka-29 Helix-B (number "23") and Ka-29RLD (number "032"). Note also the unusual camouflaged Yak-38M Forger-A in the foreground. (Archives)

A new anti-submarine warfare Helix, the Ka-27K, has a cockpit like the Ka-29's but has the undernose radar of the Ka-27. (Kamov design bureau)

The design configuration of the Mi-26 is very similar to that of its predecessor, the Mi-6, but at quite a new technological level. Possessing a maximum takeoff weight of 56,000kg, the Mi-26 can carry up to 20,000kg of payload. Its maximum level speed is 295km/h. Its range on standard internal fuel is 800km.

The IAR-330L is a Romanian-made licence version of the French AS 330 Puma medium multi-purpose helicopter. More than 170 are thought to have been manufactured for military and civil use in Brasov. About 100 of them were operated by the Romanian Air Force, and about 60-70 were exported to Pakistan, Sudan and other countries.

The fuselage side of the Mi-26 Halo showing the fairing for chaff/flare dispensers. At present these fairings are not being used and are closed, but the whole system is ready to be installed. The small, low main landing gear is seen below.

The assault version of Romanian IAR-330 Puma is armed with two forward firing 20mm cannon. The outriggers on each side of cabin can carry four unguided rocket pods and wire-guided 9M14 Malyutka (AT-3 Sagger) anti-tank missiles.

The Polish-made W-3 Sokol (Falcon) helicopter made its first flight on 16 November 1979. Production started in 1985 in Poland's WSK Swidnik plant. More than 50 were built. The Sokol's takeoff weight is 6,400kg, and its payload is 2,100kg. It has a maximum speed of 255km/h. The photo shows a Sokol of Poland's military air unit.

One proposed variant of the W-3 Sokol will be capable of transporting fourteen troops. This stretched version would be known as the W-3L Sokol Long.

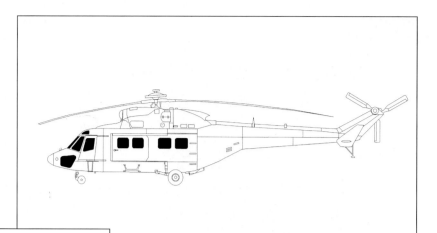

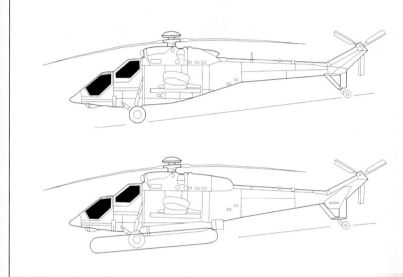

A sketch of a concept for two Polish combat helicopters, based on the Sokol's powerplant, rotors and transmission system. The W-3MS (above) is an anti-tank helicopter for army aviation; the W-3MW is a maritime strike version.

An *izdieliye* 280, later known as Mi-28 Havoc, made its maiden flight on 10 November 1992 piloted by Gurgen Karapetyan. The first prototype, number "012", was characterised by an early configuration fire control system with a multi-faceted sensor pack under the nose. An aerodynamic fairing covered the gun assembly.

Number "022", the second prototype of the Mi-28 Havoc, introduced a new nose design with a traversable turret for optical sight. The anti-tank missile radio command guidance pod is mounted on the tip of the nose.

Number "022"'s nose with an optical sight and laser range finder/target designator in a double glazed turret above the gun, with which it rotates through plus 115 degrees and minus 115 degrees. The round windows at each side of turret are designed for Forward-Looking Infrared (FLIR) and Low-Light-Level TV (LLLTV) night vision systems which, however, were never fitted to the aircraft. On the fourth prototype, these windows have already been dispensed with.

When compared with the Mi-24 Hind, the Mi-28 Havoc is a pure anti-tank helicopter, having had its center fuselage cabin removed. Note the conventional three-bladed tail rotor which was used on the first and second prototypes.

As its principal anti-tank weapon, the Mi-28 uses the new Ataka anti-tank missile or the same Shturm missile that equipped the late versions of the Mi-24. This photo shows a cluster of eight Shturm tube-launched missiles and an B-8V-20 rocket pod on the port wing of "022".

An engine nacelle on number "022" prototype shows the old type of infrared suppression cool air mixer above the engine exhaust. Located above and to the rear of the engine, it directed the exhaust rearward.

Mi-28 "042" in flight.

The third prototype, number "032", incorporates a new "X"-pattern tail rotor and a heavily reconfigured suppressor/mixer over the engine exhaust.

The Mi-28 has a crew of two: a weapon systems officer in the front cockpit and a pilot behind, sitting on the elevated seat. The crew compartment is protected by titanium and ceramic armor and armored glass. The turreted cannon of the Mi-28 is a derivative of the 2A42 cannon originally mounted on the BMP-2 armored infantry vehicle. Its field of fire is plus 10 degrees and minus 40 degrees in elevation, and 115 degrees to either side of the fuselage centerline in azimuth.

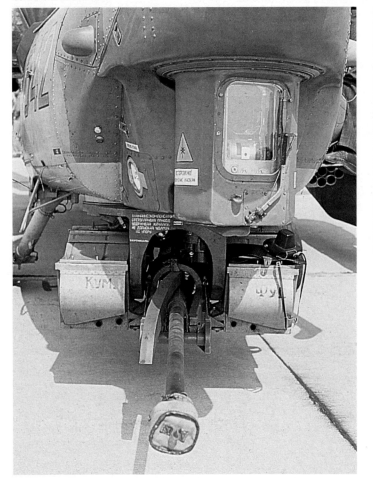

The helicopter carriers 300 rounds of ammunition in two containers on either side of the cannon. The two ammunition boxes permit the selection of either high-explosive or armor piercing ammunition.

The chin mounted electro-optics turret contains the target acquisition sight and the laser range finder. The munition boxes seen in the lower part of photo bear the carelessly painted inscriptions of "Kum" (the abbreviation of *kumulativnyi* - armor piercing) and "Fug" (which stands for *fugasnyi* - high explosive).

A look into the gunner's cockpit. The TV screen with thick anti-reflection rubber cover occupies the central position, the missile control sight is mounted on the starboard side of the cockpit.

The central position in the pilot's cockpit is occupied by TV screen and head-up-display is installed above.

The pilot's cockpit. Both Mi-28's cockpits are less spacious when compared with Ka-50.

This view of the middle part of fuselage of prototype number "042" shows the weapons carrying wing, engine nacelles and landing gear.

The first three prototypes had no infrared jammer, nor were there any fitting for the chaff/flare dispensers. Large fairings at the wing tips of the fourth prototype contain UV-26 chaff/flare dispensers and probably also some other equipment. The countermeasure dispensers are covered in this photo.

The Klimov TV3-117 engines are much more widely spaced apart from one another than on the Mi-24. This reduces the likelihood of a single missile or projectile explosion damaging both engines. The housing in the center is the aircraft's AI-9V auxiliary power unit (APU).

The new exhaust suppressor/mixer is outboard the engine. This draws in outside air, mixing it with the exhaust gas and deflecting it downward.

The conventional three-blade tail rotor in the third and fourth prototypes is replaced by an "X"-type comprising two independent two-blade rotors on the same shaft.

The main landing gear. The Mi-28 Havoc has the non-retractable tailwheel style of landing gear, with a single wheel on each unit.

The small tail wheel has a trapezoidal IFF antenna in front of it. The side warnings mean "Danger - turning rotor".

The Mi-40 combat transport helicopter is based on the dynamic system of Mi-28 Havoc. When fully loaded, the Mi-40 will be armed with eight anti-tank tube-launched missiles, four rocket pods, and will carry ten troops. Its first flight is expected to be in 1995.

In the seventies and eighties, the Kamov design bureau prepared a series of designs of combat helicopters. The picture shows a non-produced V-50 combat transport helicopter that was designed for the Navy. It was eventually replaced by Ka-29 helicopter.

A Ka-25F combat helicopter design which lost out to its competitor, the Mi-24 Hind, in 1967.

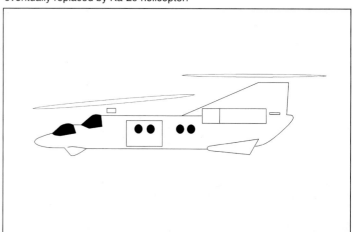

An extraordinary design of Kamov V-100 heavy attack helicopter was proposed in the eighties. It was to be armed with 3,000kg of bombs/rockets, two guns, and two Kh-25 anti-radar/anti-ship missiles.

The very first design of Kamov V-80 fighter helicopter dates back to 1970.

A design of the V-60 light fighter helicopter, which was proposed in the mid-eighties and based on the Ka-126. The V-60 was to be armed with a 30mm cannon and four anti-aircraft missiles.

The "010" is the first prototype of the new Kamov V-80 (or *izdieliye* 800) helicopter. On 17 June 1982, Nikolai Bezdetnov made the first hovering with the V-80, and on 27 July Yevgeniy Laryushin made the first full circle. Note the painting imitating a two-seater helicopter used to fool possible unwanted observers. (Kamov design bureau)

One of the early "paper" variants of the V-80. Note the different wings and tail as compared to the real Hokum.

53

The "012" is the third prototype, now ready for aerodynamic tests. It has no fire control system and lacks a cannon at the starboard side of the fuselage. The big boxes suspended under the wings contain the measuring equipment. The cameras for recording the behavior of rotors in flight are installed on the neighboring pylons.

One of the first production Hokums. After the start of serial manufacturing in the summer of 1991 at the Arsenyev plant near Vladivostok, the helicopter was named Ka-50 Hokum. (Kamov design bureau)

A Ka-50 c/n 01003, the third example of the first production series, was displayed in Farnborough during its international debut in September 1992. This photo was made after the helicopter's return from Farnborough. The Ka-50 is sitting on front of the hangar on the Kamov design bureau's airfield.

The entire machine is in black with Russian tricolor flags on the engine nacelles. A picture of a wolf's head has been painted on the top of tailfin along with the caption "Werewolf" - the export name of Ka-50. Its small bit of color consists of a red triangle with a "Ka-50" caption on the vertical tailfins, a small number "020" at the bottom of the cockpit and the English caption "Army Attack Helicopter" on the port side of fuselage.

A side-view of "Werewolf".

The Kamov designers have configured the Ka-50 helicopter with two coaxial, contra-rotating three-bladed rotors. The rotor blades have a diameter of 14.5m. The design for these rotors is entirely original to the Kamov design bureau and typical of their ingenuity.

The Ka-50 Hokum is unique in the world. It is the only singlecrew combat helicopter. It is also the first production helicopter equipped with a pilot's ejection seat. The K-37 Zvezda/Severin rocket ejection seat was specially designed for the helicopter. Georgiy Shishkin, Kamov's test pilot, is seated in cockpit.

The armament is carried on four underwing pylons, each having a capacity of 500kg. The basic anti-tank armament consists of Vikhr (Whirlwind, AT-9 in NATO) missiles. The Vikhr is a 60kg supersonic missile with a maximum range of 10km. The missile is operated by a combination of radio command and laser guidance. The clusters of Vikhr missiles are carried on the pods with an adjustable lower edge; they can be lowered by 10 degrees downwards thus reducing the length of missile path to the target.

The 2A42 cannon, seen also on the Mi-28, is installed in the lower part of the starboard side of the fuselage. The movable barrel is controlled by the helicopter weapons control system. Five hundred rounds of munitions are stored in two boxes in the lower part of fuselage.

The large window of the Shkval (Squall) optics-LLLTV (Low-Level-Light TV) aiming system is situated under the Hokum's nose.

UV-26 chaff/flare dispensers with 26mm PPI-26 flares or PPR-26 radar decoys are installed inside a large fairing at the wing tips. The flares are launched automatically during the attack according to a programmed sequence.

The Ka-50 is powered by two St. Petersburg/Klimov TV3-117VK turboshaft engines. These engines were also used in the Mi-28 and the whole former generation of transport and combat helicopters. The air intakes are equipped with dust filters.

Each helicopter seems to have a different means by which the crew enters the cockpit; ladders or steps are commonly seen on Russian aircraft. On this helicopter, the ladders have been replaced by a wide platform on the port side of the fuselage.

The tricycle undercarriage is fully retractable in order to reduce aerodynamic drag as well as radar signature. The main leg looks delicate but the experts say that it can endure three times greater the impact against the ground than the landing gear of former helicopters.

Here is a look into a full-scale mock-up of the cockpit of a V-80. The cockpit looks much like that of the Ka-50, and even includes the changes that were made in that helicopter's cockpit.

The inside of the Ka-50 cabin resembles an aircraft's cockpit. The central area is occupied by the TV screen of the Shkval system, and its thick anti-reflection rubber cover. The Head-Up-Display is installed on top and the cartographic indicator displaying the current position of the helicopter is at the right hand side.

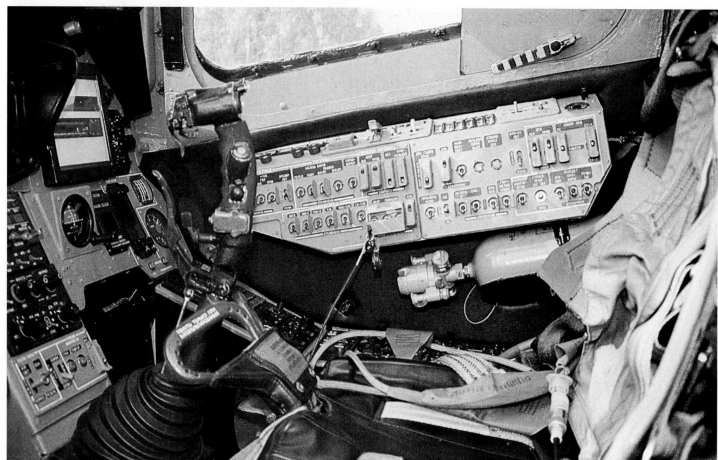

A close-up view of a control stick, the pilot's ejection seat and a starboard instrument panel.

A normal takeoff weight for the Ka-50 Hokum is 9,800kg; the maximum is 10,800kg. It has a maximum level flight speed of 270km/h; in a shallow dive it is up to 350km/h. A normal range is 500km. The g-limit is 3.0.

An Mi-34 Hermit light trainer helicopter.

The Ka-37 is a light pilotless helicopter which made its first flight in late 1992. It has a weight of 250kg. In military applications, the Ka-37 can carry reconnaissance or jamming system.

A full-scale mock-up of the Ka-62 helicopter of the 1,500kg payload class. The first flight of the Ka-62 is expected to be in 1993.

A full-scale mock-up of the new generation Mi-38 medium transport/assault helicopter. It will replace the Mi-8/Mi-17 Hip.

The Mi-46 is the proposed flying-crane variant of the Mi-26. (Mil design bureau)

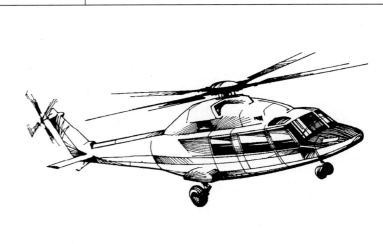

A concept of an Mi-54 multi-purpose helicopter of the Mi-2 Hoplite class. (Mil design bureau)

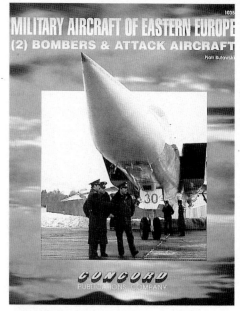

1028 Military Aircraft of Eastern Europe: (1)
Fighters & interceptors
Piotr Butowski

1032 Maple Flag
Mike YReyno

1035 Military Aircraft of Eastern Europe: (2)
Bombers & Attack Aircraft
Piotr Butowski

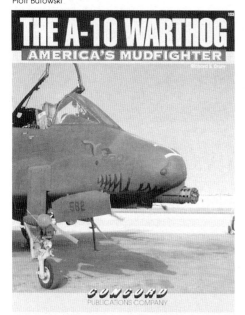

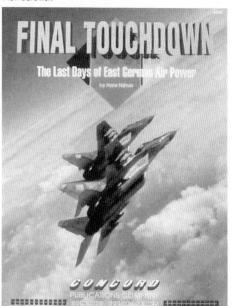

1037 A-10 Warthog: America's Mudfighter
Richard S. Drury

3003 Red Star over Europe
Marcus Fülber

4003 Final Touchdown: The Last Days of East
German Air Power
Hans Nijhuis

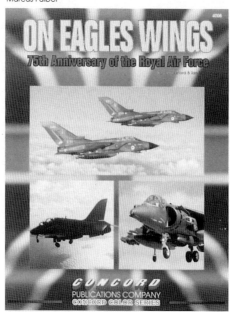

4006 Carrier Air Wing Six
Yves Debay & James Hill

4008 On Eagles Wings:
75th Anniversary of the Royal Air Force
Tom Wakeford & Ian Rentoul

CONCORD
PUBLICATIONS COMPANY